knit

first stitch / first scarf

by Quince & Company

Illustrated by Leila Raabe
Photographed by Pam Allen

quince&co.

Knit
first stitch / first scarf

Copyright 2016 by Quince & Co

Cover and book design by Jennifer S. Muller

ISBN 978-0-9861039-7-1

Library of Congress Control Number

Printed in the U.S.

Published by Quince & Co
142 High Street, Suite 220, Portland, Maine 04101

Knitting is a craft as old as written history. It requires yarn and needles, patience, practice, and thought. For a small investment of time and care, its rewards are many. When you knit, you always have a companion, a project ready to pick up when you sit down. Knitting lends itself to simple creative pleasures. It invites you to explore color and its relationships, to create textures, to make garments that warm and comfort you. Knitting allows you to run soft fibers through your fingers, fibers that often come from plants and animals that require open fields and range to grow and graze. As you develop your skills, you experience the quiet joy that comes with competence and understanding.

Perhaps I wax too strongly on the joys of knitting. But pick up your needles and yarn, learn to create stitches, watch a swatch, a scarf, a hat come to life, and you may very well agree with me.

Pam Allen

Bird's Egg

Damson

Audouin

Kumlien's Gull

Carrie's Yellow

Welcome to knitting!

If you want to learn to knit, look no further. This small book provides a step-by-step guide to knitting basics, plus two patterns for easy-to-knit scarves. In *Knit*, we show you in detail how to cast on stitches, knit them, purl them, and bind them off. In addition, we explain how to work a variety of knit-and-purl stitch patterns, how to weave in ends and block your finished piece, and how to read and understand a knitting pattern. Most important, we show you how to fix your mistakes. No worries, we all make them, beginner and experienced knitters alike.

First, a quick word about what knitting is.

Knitting is a method of making a stretchy fabric using a continuous strand of yarn and two dowel-like needles. Knitted fabric is made of stitches, connected to each other, that run horizontally in rows across your piece. As you knit, you'll see that stitches are also arranged in columns, each new stitch is pulled through and stacked on the stitch from the previous row.

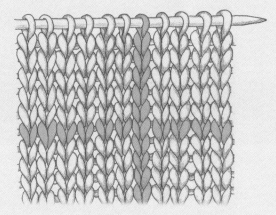

The foundation stitches are held in a row on the left-hand needle. To knit, you use the right-hand (working) needle to create and pull a loop of yarn, called a stitch, through another loop (stitch) held at the tip end of the left-hand needle. The new stitch is formed on the right-hand needle and the old stitch is slipped off the holding needle. When all the stitches have been worked from the left-hand needle, and the right-hand needle holds the new stitches, the needles are switched, and the now-empty left-hand needle becomes the right-hand working needle.

Like any new skill, knitting may feel awkward at first. But before you know it, you'll be cruising along. Your fingers will start to do things automatically, and you'll watch your stitches become more and more even and your handsome practice scarf grow and grow. By the time you're binding off the last row, you'll be thinking about your next project.

Note: If you're left-handed, this book is for you. Left-handed knitters can easily work from directions for their right-handed friends. The only difference in actual practice is that if you're left-handed, you'll drive the movements with your left hand, not with your right. It doesn't make a whit of difference in the final project. So no need to worry about reversing any of the instructions.

Getting Started

Like all crafts, knitting requires tools and materials, but all you need to get started are a ball of yarn and a pair of knitting needles.

Yarn and needles

For beginning practice, a wool yarn in a light, easy-to-see color is best. Wool is more elastic and forgiving than plant fibers, such as cotton and linen, or acrylics. A medium-weight yarn will make practicing easy. Look for a worsted or Aran-weight yarn (see page 42 for more information on yarn).

Yarn comes in a ball, ready to use, or in a skein (pronounced skane). A skein is a closed loop of yarn twisted and folded in on itself. Choose your yarn first and then choose your needles. Often, the label on your yarn will suggest an appropriate needle size.

Needles come in different sizes, determined by their circumference, and they come in different lengths. The larger the needle's circumference, the larger the stitch, or loop, it makes. Thick yarns need big needles to make a pliable, soft fabric. If your needles are too small for your yarn, the resulting fabric (scarf, hat, sweater) will be dense and stiff. If the needles are too big, the fabric will be loose and sloppy.

How to wind a ball

If your yarn is packaged in a skein, before you can cast on and start knitting, you have to convert it into a ball.

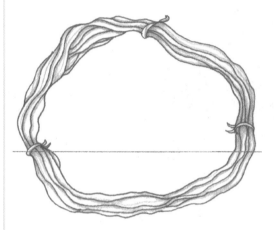

Untwist the skein from its pretzel shape and look for the short yarn ties that keep the loop contained. These two or three little ties hold the looped yarn together as it goes through the dyeing process. Until you cut those, your skein will stay nicely organized.

Step 1: Secure your skein

Before snipping the ties, place the opened skein over a chair back, a willing helper's stretched-out arms, or simply drape it over your knees. The goal is to unwind the skein in an orderly way as you wind your ball, otherwise, you'll quickly have a tangled mess on your hands.

Once your skein is secured, find the yarn ties that run perpendicular to the skein. With scissors, carefully cut these holding strands. You'll find that one of these cuts reveals the ends of your looped skein. Now you're ready to go.

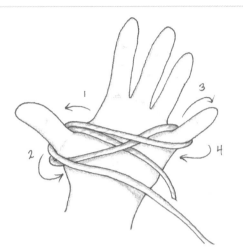

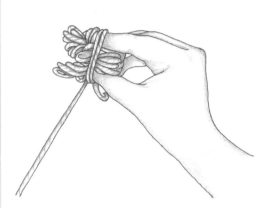

Step 2: Make a butterfly

With the tail of the yarn draped lightly in the palm of your left hand, make a figure-eight around thumb and pinky. Continue winding 8's 10 to 15 times to make a butterfly.

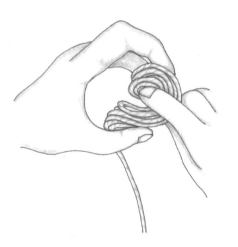

Then grab the 8's in the center where the strands cross, slip the loops from thumb and little finger, and fold the 8's in half, making a little bundle.

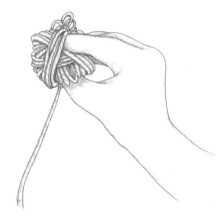

Step 3: Start winding

Holding the folded 8's in one hand, begin to wind the yarn gently around the little bundle. Start by winding perpendicular to the strands, then shift the position of your little yarn package and continue to wrap.

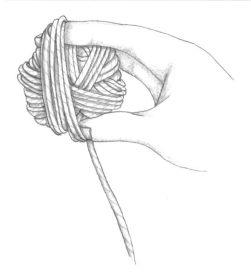

Be sure to wind the yarn over your thumb or fingers every time you pass the yarn around. Winding over your fingers provides a little breathing room for the yarn so that it isn't stretched tight in the balling process. As you wrap, switch directions now and then to create a ball-like form.

When you come to the end of the skein, you'll have a ball of yarn to admire.

How to cast on

Before you can begin knitting proper, you have to create the initial row of stitches on one of your needles. Making the foundation row is called casting on.

There are several different ways to cast on. We like the long-tail cast on, shown here, because it's easy to do and makes a stable, tidy edge.

To begin, from the tail end of your yarn ball, measure out about an inch for every stitch you'll cast on (20 stitches is a good number to practice on), and a few extra inches for good measure, about 25"-30" total. At this point on your strand, make your first stitch, a slip knot, to secure the yarn to the needle.

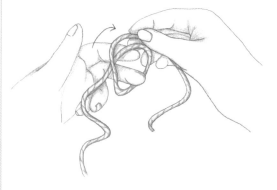

Step 1: Make a slipknot
a. Make a smallish loop, about the size of a silver dollar, overlapping the tail end on the working yarn.

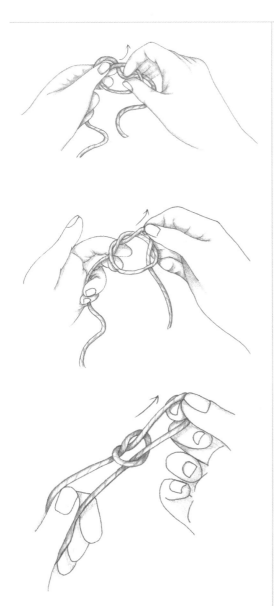

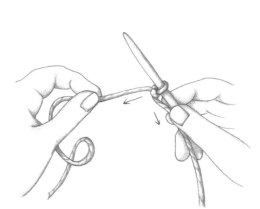

c. Put the slipknot on your needle. Snug the knot by gently pulling on both ends.

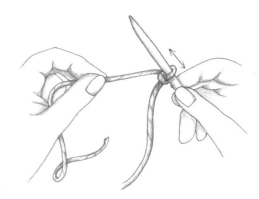

b. Reach through the loop, grab the tail, and pull it through the loop.

Holding the loop just pulled through, pull gently on the yarn ends until the pulled-loop shrinks a little. This is your slipknot.

The knot should be firm to the needle, not too tight, not too loose. As you slide this loop back and forth on the needle, you should feel it in contact with the needle, but you shouldn't feel any resistance. It should glide easily, not sloppily.

Voila!—your first stitch. When you count your stitches, this slipknot counts as one stitch.

Step 2: Make more stitches on your needle
Take a look at the strands hanging from the
slipknot snugged on your needle. The working
yarn is the end that comes from your ball. Position
the strands so the working yarn is on the right
and the tail is on the left. Hold the needle and the
working yarn in your right hand, the tail in your
left, a few inches away from the needle, with a
little tension on it and thumb on top of yarn.

a. Create a loop by rotating your thumb under
the tail end from behind, then up so your thumb
is parallel with the needle and the yarn is looped
around it.

c. Secure this position by switching the needle
to your left hand while it's still in the loop on
your thumb and, with your right hand, wrap
the working yarn counter-clockwise around the
needle and sandwich it between the thumb and
the needle in your left hand.

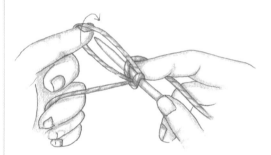

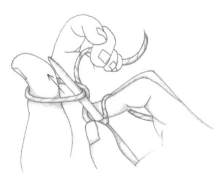

b. Insert the tip of the needle upward into the
loop formed around your thumb.

d. Now, grasp the needle again with your right
hand and with your thumb lift the loop of yarn
that's been sitting on it, bring it up and back and
over the tip of the needle.

Pull gently on the tail end to firm up your (second)
stitch. Remember: not too tight and not too loose.

Repeat the process from **a** through **d** until you have 20 stitches on your needle. Now you're ready to start knitting proper. But before moving on, take a moment to examine your cast-on stitches.

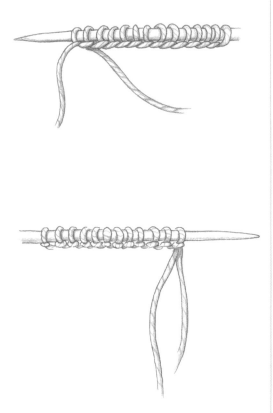

Holding the needle with the tip pointing left, you'll see a series of diagonal strands at the base of each stitch. Turn the needle around, tip to the right, and you'll see a tidy row of bumps along the needle's edge.

How to knit

The word 'knit' refers to both a specific kind of stitch (the knit stitch) and also the general act of making stitches of all kinds with yarn and needles. Here we show you the basic knit stitch.

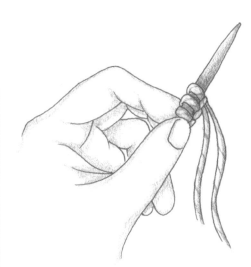

Hold your needle with its cast-on stitches in the left hand, needle tip pointing to the right. A comfortable way to position the needle in your hand is to hold it in a very loose fist, with forefinger and thumb perched near the tip, the first stitch about an inch from the pointed end.

Note that the first stitch on the needle, the one at the tip end, is also the last stitch you cast on. It has two strands hanging from it, the tail and the working yarn. Ignore the tail, you're done with it for now. From here, use only the working yarn, extending from the ball. The needle holding the ready-to-work stitches is called the left-hand (LH) needle.

With the needle holding the cast-on stitches in your left hand, first stitch about an inch from the tip, and the empty needle in your right hand, you're ready to knit your first stitch.

Step 2: Wrap the working yarn counter-clockwise around the empty needle and sandwich it between the two needles.

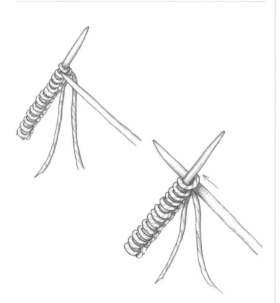

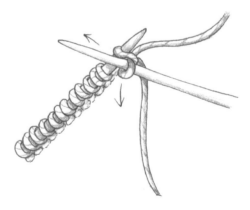

Step 1: With the right-hand (RH) needle tip positioned to the left of the first stitch, maneuver the tip through the first stitch, bringing it out behind the LH needle—your needle tips will form a rough X-shape.

Step 3: Put a slight bit of tension on the yarn with the right hand and, as you slide your RH needle down (or LH needle up), bring the strand wrapped around the RH needle through that first stitch on the LH needle; there is now a loop on the RH needle.

Step 4: Slide the old loop gently all the way to the LH needle tip—then right OFF the needle. TADA—your first knitted stitch!

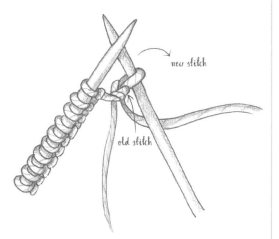

If you'd like a little help remembering these four steps, you can repeat the rhyme below which corresponds to the steps above:

In through the window
(insert RH needle into stitch on LH needle)

Run around the back
(wrap working yarn around RH needle)

Out through the window
(bring wrap through old stitch on LH needle)

Off jumps jack.
(slide old stitch off needle)

Or make your own version.

Tip: Adjusting the tension on your stitches so they're even gets easier with practice. If you need to slightly pull on the yarn end after finishing a stitch, go right ahead. But don't over do it. You want your stitches to be snug to the needle, not tight. (Tight stitches are common when you're learning to knit.) Aim instead for stitches that are relaxed and easy, but not sloppy. Remember, they should gently hug the needle when you slide them along, but they should glide easily.

Continue Steps 1-4 until you've worked all the stitches on the left hand needle. You've just completed Row 1.

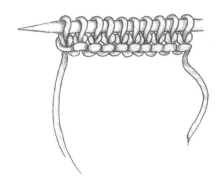

Before turning your needle to place it in the left hand, take a look at your first row. You'll see a series of small bumps from the cast on, and just above them, a series of little V's, your first stitches.

To work Row 2, the next row, turn the right-hand needle with its newly made stitches and hold it in your left hand, needle tip pointing right. This is now your left-hand needle. Look familiar? The empty needle is now your right-hand, working needle. The working yarn hangs from the first stitch on your left-hand needle. Repeat Steps 1-4 above until you've worked all the stitches on the left-hand needle.

As you continue to practice knitting, take note of the two pointers below that will help you avoid common beginner mistakes.

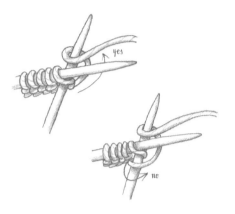

1) Before knitting each knit stitch, be sure the working yarn is in back of your work, not in front. If it's in front, the yarn will go over the RH needle and create an extra stitch.

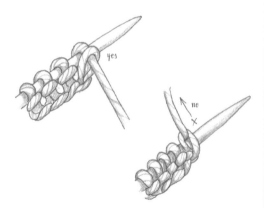

2) You may be faced with an oversized stitch at the beginning of a row. Resist the temptation to pull the yarn over the back of the needle to make it look neater, as this creates an extra stitch. Fear not, as you continue knitting, you will learn how to make those end stitches as tidy as the rest of the stitches in your row.

Continue to practice knitting until you feel comfortable with the moves. Then take a look at what you've made.

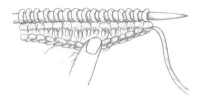

To see the individual stitches in your knitted piece, slightly stretch your fabric vertically. The stitches you made with the right side facing you form a V shape. The stitches you formed when the other side was facing you, appear as little bumps. When you knit every row, the fabric you create is called garter stitch. You can always identify garter stitch by its pronounced horizontal texture. Although we say 'right side' and 'wrong side' when we refer to a knitting project, garter stitch looks the same from each side and is, therefore, reversible. Garter stitch makes wonderful, cushy and versatile fabric. If you can cast on, knit, and bind off (next page), you have all the skills needed to make Puck's Scarf (page 32).

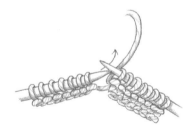

Tip: If possible, always complete a row before setting aside your knitting. If you stop in the middle of a row and can't remember which needle is which, check the stitches at the tips of the needles. The RH working needle always has the stitch with the working yarn strand extending from it.

How to bind off

When you've reached the end of your practice piece, you need to bind off your stitches to secure them. Leave a tail at least three times the width of your piece before starting the last (bind off) row.

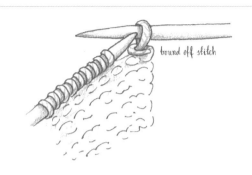

bound off stitch

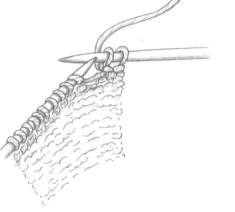

Step 1: Knit two stitches (K2).

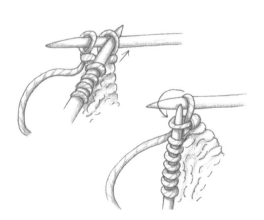

Step 2: With your LH needle, pull the first stitch worked on the RH needle over the second stitch and off the needle. You've bound off one stitch; there is one stitch left on the RH needle.

Step 3: Knit the next stitch on the LH needle (two stitches are again on the RH needle).

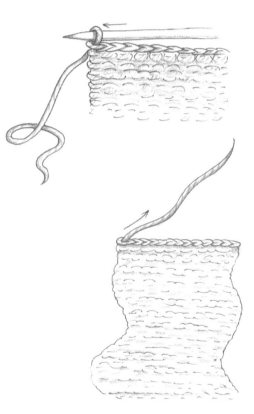

Repeat Steps 2 and 3 until you have one stitch left on the RH needle. Cut the yarn, leaving a 6″ tail and pull this tail through the last stitch.

How to purl

To make smooth knitted fabric, called stock-inette stitch, or ribbing with its strong vertical lines, or any of the myriad other knitting patterns, you need to learn to make a knitted stitch backwards. This is called purling. Purling is knitting from the back side of the knit stitch.

To purl, hold the needle with the stitches in your left hand and the empty needle in your right.

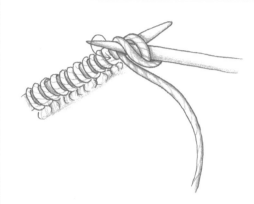

Step 2: Wrap the working yarn counter-clock-wise around the empty needle and sandwich it between the two needles.

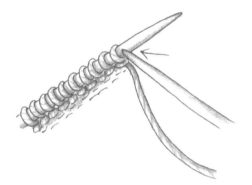

Step 1: With the RH needle tip to the right of the first stitch, maneuver the tip through the first stitch, keeping it to the front of the LH needle.

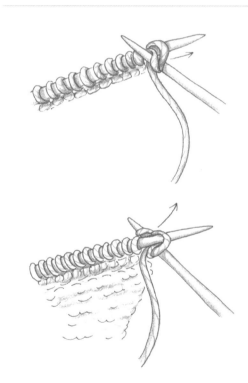

Step 3: Put a slight bit of tension on the yarn with the right hand, and as you slide your RH needle down (or LH needle up), push the strand

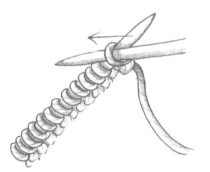

The needle tips will form a rough X-shape, same as when you knit, only this time the RH needle is in front of the LH needle.

wrapped around the RH needle through that first stitch. This time, it's more of a front-to-back motion—your RH needle will end up behind the LH needle after you've pushed the working yarn through. There is now a loop on the RH needle.

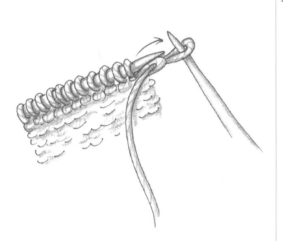

Step 4: Then, same as knitting, slide the old loop gently to the tip of the LH needle—then right OFF the needle. There you have it, one purl stitch!

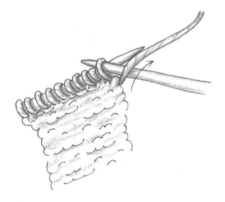

Continue Steps 1-4 until you've worked all the stitches on the LH needle. You've just purled one row.

Note: When you come to the end of a purl row, and you turn your needle to get ready to work the next row, notice that the working yarn extending from the last stitch is angled toward the back of the work. To purl the first stitch, bring the yarn forward so the RH needle is behind the working yarn when you insert it into the first stitch.

As you work you'll see that the fabric you make when you purl every row looks just like knit-every-row fabric. Purling every row is another way to work garter stitch.

Both swatches are worked in garter stitch. The one above was made by knitting every row, the one below by purling every row. Either knitting or purling, when you work the same stitch on every row, you make garter stitch. It's easy to spot by the strong horizontal lines.

These swatches show both sides of stockinette stitch, made by alternating one knitted row with one purled row. The smooth side is stockinette stitch proper, and usually the right side of the fabric. The bumpy side is called reverse stockinette stitch. Sometimes the bumpy side is used as the right side of the piece.

Top to bottom:
Welting
One-by-one Ribbing
Double Ribbing

Mixing it up–basic stitch patterns

Once you can knit and purl, you can combine these two stitches in endless ways. Here are some basic knit-and-purl stitch patterns that you can use to make a simple scarf.

Garter stitch
You already know how to do this. When you knit every row, or purl every row, you create garter stitch (page 20).

You can recognize garter stitch by its distinctive horizontal ridges.

Stockinette stitch
(St st)
Row 1: (RS) Knit all the stitches.

Row 2: Purl all the stitches.
Repeat these two rows to make stockinette stitch (page 21).

Do you see how one side is smooth and one side is bumpy? Look closely at the smooth side. Under each stitch on your needle, you'll see a column of Vs, each V is a stitch made by knitting on the right (smooth) side of the fabric (RS), or purling on the wrong side (WS). Turn your work around and you'll see that a column of bumps descends from each stitch on the needle. These bumps represent a stitch knitted on the RS, and a stitch purled on the WS.

Reverse stockinette stitch
(rev St st)
When you make the bumpy side of stockinette stitch the right side of your garment, then the pattern is called reverse stockinette stitch. The instructions would direct you to purl across one row, then knit across the next row. These two rows make reverse stockinette stitch (page 21).

Welting
Rows 1 and 2: Knit all stitches.

Rows 3 and 4: Purl all stitches.
Repeat these four rows to make welts (page 22).

Notice that every time you knit on a wrong side row, you create a row of bumps on the right side, same as if you'd purled on a right side. You can play with the size of your welts by knitting or purling on the right or wrong side as needed.

One-by-one ribbing
(work over an even number of stitches)
Ribbing is what happens when you alternate a knit stitch with a purl stitch on a single row. This creates columns of knit stitches and purl stitches. Ribbing is reversible.

Row 1: *Knit one stitch (K1), bring the working yarn between the needles to the front, purl one stitch (p1); repeat from * (the beginning) to the end of the row. Ribbing is reversible.
Repeat Row 1 as many times as you like for one-by-one ribbing (page 22).

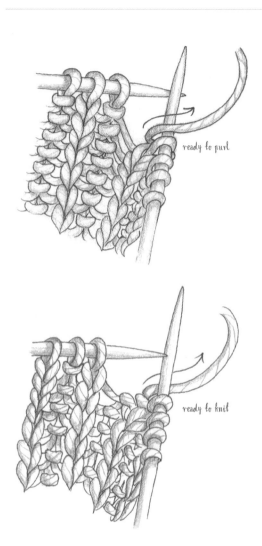

ready to purl

ready to knit

Note: Whenever you go from a knit stitch to a purl stitch or vice versa, you need to reposition the working yarn. When you go from a knit stitch to a purl, bring the yarn between the needles to the front of your work where it's ready to work a purl stitch. When you go from working a purl stitch to a knit stitch, bring the yarn between the needles to the back of your work.

Double ribbing
(work over a multiple of four stitches)
In standard one-by-one ribbing, you alternate one knit stitch with one purl stitch. In double ribbing, you alternate two knit stitches with two purl stitches. For double ribbing, you need a multiple of four stitches.

Row 1: *K2, p2; repeat from * (the beginning) to the end of the row.
Repeat Row 1 for double ribbing (page 22).

Alternating knits and purls allows for all kinds of rib patterns. Try alternating three knit stitches with three purls for 3x3 ribbing. Ribbing doesn't have to be symmetrical. Try casting on a mulitple of six stitches and knitting two stitches, then purling four. Repeat this sequence across all the stitches. On the next row, knit four, then purl two across. Then check what it looks like from both sides of your knitted piece.

Seed stitch
(work over an even number of stitches)
This is another stitch pattern that alternates knit stitches with purls. But this time the knit stitches and purls are staggered. Instead of making knit/purl columns, seed stitch creates a checkerboard pattern. Like ribbing, seed stitch and its variations are reversible.

Row 1: *K1, p1; repeat from * (the beginning) to the end of the row.

Row 2: *P1, k1; repeat from * (the beginning) to the end of the row.
Repeat these two rows for seed stitch (page 23).

Moss stitch
(work over an even number of stitches)
Moss stitch is a little expansion on seed stitch—instead of staggering the knit/purl combination every row, you stagger it every other row.

Rows 1 and 2: *K1, p1; repeat from *(the beginning) to the end of the row.

Rows 3 and 4: *P1, k1; repeat from *(the beginning) to the end of the row.
Repeat these four rows for moss stitch (page 23).

Double seed stitch
(work over a multiple of four stitches)
Double seed stitch is another variation on seed stitch. In this version, you alternate two knitted stitches with two purls, and stagger them every other row.

Rows 1 and 2: *K2, p2; rep from * (the beginning) to the end of the row.

Rows 3 and 4: *P2, k2; rep from * (the beginning) to the end of the row.
Repeat these four rows for double seed stitch (page 23).

A few more techniques

If you can knit and purl, you're well on your way to being a proficient knitter. Here are a few more techniques to master for smooth sailing in your new craft.

How to join a new ball of yarn
Whenever possible, join a new ball of yarn at the edge of your work, rather than in the middle of a row. Each row of knitting uses a length of yarn approximately double the width of your piece. So when you see that you don't have enough yarn to finish the next row, it's time to join a new ball of yarn to your work.

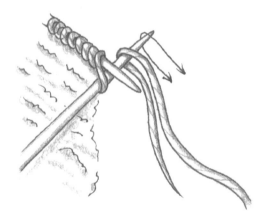

Insert your RH needle into the first stitch on the LH needle as usual. Lay the strand of the new ball in between the two needles, with a good 6-8″ tail dangling behind the needle, and the working yarn in front.

Secure the new strand with your right hand while you complete the stitch as usual, pulling the working yarn through the stitch on the LH needle. To make your new yarn secure, tie the new tail temporarily to the tail of the first skein at the edge of your work.

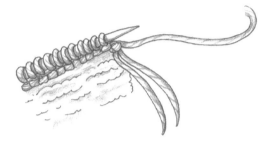

When you've finished your scarf, you'll undo the knot and neatly weave in the ends (page 29).

How to fix mistakes

As you practice knitting, you may notice places in your work where the stitches don't look quite right. They may look uneven, or a hole may have appeared a few rows down; perhaps your scarf is growing horizontally as well as vertically.

These glitches are learning mistakes. Don't give up. We all make them. What to do? There are several ways to remedy specific mistakes, but the easiest way to get back to pretty knitting at this early stage is to get comfortable with unraveling. Never be discouraged by unraveling. Think about it. How many times in life can you go back and fix something in a way that it might never have happened? Not many. Knitters are lucky, they do it all the time.

Tinking (un-knitting) one stitch at a time

If your mistake or wonky stitch is only a few rows below your needle, you can pick out all the stitches you've worked, one by one, until you've unpicked to and through the problem area. You can restart knitting again from that point.

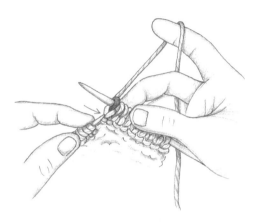

Step 1: With the needle holding stitches in your right hand, insert the tip of the LH needle front to back into the center of the stitch below the one on the RH needle.

Step 2: With the stitch below captured on the LH needle, slide the upper stitch off the RH needle and tug gently on the working yarn to unravel the upper stitch.
You've unraveled a single stitch, but the stitch below is secure.

Repeat Steps 1 and 2, undoing stitches, until you've unknitted the problem. Then begin fresh.

Ripping back

If you've worked several inches before noticing a problem area, the quickest way to get back to the mistake is to rip out a row at a time, rather than stitch by stitch.

Step 1: Slide all of the stitches off of your needle.

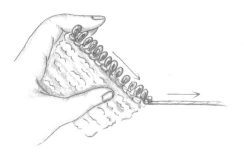

Step 2: Pull on the working yarn to undo your stitches.
Continue pulling out stitches until you've pulled out the problem stitches. Then continue to rip out until the end of the problem row.

Step 3: To place the stitches back on your needle, hold the knitted piece with the working yarn on the right. Insert the tip of the needle, front to back, into the first stitch at the left edge. Continue to catch each stitch from front to back until all stitches are on the needle. Or simply tink the last row, ripping one stitch at a time as you insert your needle.

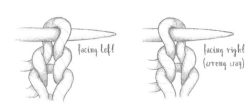

Note: Why do we specify front to back? Because it's important to keep your stitches oriented in the proper way on your needle. Stitches should face left, not right.

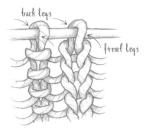

Also, stitches can be thought to have front legs and back legs. The front leg is on your side of the needle and the back leg is on the far side. The legs should not cross at the bottom.

If the stitch is positioned the wrong way, facing right, when you knit it, the legs will cross and you will have a twisted stitch.

You can fix a twisted stitch if you catch it on your needle by untwisting it and putting it back on the needle facing left, the correct orientation.

Finishing your knitted project

If, after you've bound off your last stitch, your knitted piece doesn't look quite like you'd imagined—stitches are uneven, odd puckers appear, the edges wave in and out—not to worry. Finishing to the rescue.

How to weave in ends

To hide your yarn tails, you'll need a needle with a large eye and a blunt end, often called a tapestry needle.

Some stitch patterns are reversible, for example, garter, rib, and seed stitch patterns look the same on each side. Choose the side that looks best for your right side.

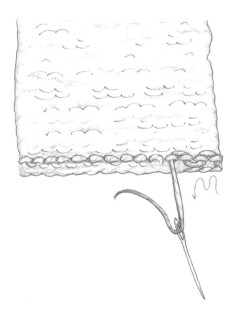

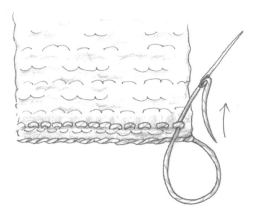

Step 1: Lay your piece flat, wrong side facing up, and thread one of your tails onto the tapestry needle.

Step 2: Using the tapestry needle, begin to thread your tail up and down through the strands in the fabric.

Continue weaving in the tail through a few more stitches. No need to weave in the whole tail. A few passes will suffice to secure the yarn end. Don't pull the tail too tightly, or you will end up with puckers in the fabric.

Now, give your scarf a gentle stretch in different directions to relax the stitches and work the end in.

Step 3: Using a small pair of scissors, carefully trim the tail close to the surface of your knitting, leaving about ½".

How to block

Here is where the magic happens. Blocking with steam or wetting, then drying, will even out wonky stitches and allow you to straighten edges and generally adjust your knitting so it looks lovely.

How to steam block your piece

Step 1: Lay your scarf out on a flat surface massaging it to the desired finished measurements, if possible. If you lay it out on your mattress, you can pin edges as needed. Place a thin towel (a linen or cotton dish towel is good) over your work. It can be dry or damp.

Step 2: Hold a steaming iron a few inches above your piece letting the steam penetrate. Do not put the iron directly onto the surface of your knitting or the towel.

Allow the knitted piece to dry and cool completely before picking it up or moving it.

Knitting from a pattern

Knitted gauge is the number of stitches and rows per inch in your knitted piece. Gauge is given, usually measured and recorded over four inches, at the beginning of a knitting pattern. Because everyone knits a little differently, and your stitches might be a little larger or smaller than the pattern's sample knitter, it's important to check your gauge before starting a pattern.

How to knit a gauge swatch

To check your stitch gauge, you need to knit a small square, called a gauge swatch, using the exact yarn, needles and stitch pattern you've lined up for your project. Cast on the number of stitches given for four inches in the pattern, plus another eight stitches, and knit in the designated stitch pattern until your swatch is 4-5″ tall. Bind off.

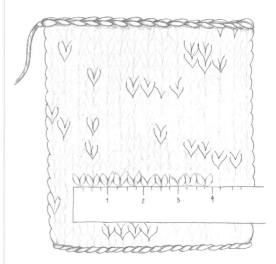

Lay your swatch on a flat surface. Steam it lightly, if you plan to block your finished piece. Using a stiff ruler, and starting four stitches from the edge, measure 4″ across your knitting. Count the number of stitches in those 4″.

Then compare your numbers to those in your pattern.

What to do if you don't get gauge

If you have fewer stitches in your swatch gauge than called for, try a smaller needle. If you have more stitches in your swatch gauge than called for, try a larger needle.

Getting exact gauge isn't all that important when you're making a scarf, which can vary widthwise by an inch or so without major consequences. However, if you're making a sweater that you want to match to a pattern's specific measurements, checking your gauge is vital. If your gauge is off by even a little over a single stitch, your sweater will be off by several inches when it's complete.

How to read (and understand) a knitting pattern

Knitting patterns can stump a new (and sometimes an experienced) knitter. They're written in truncated sentences and peppered with unfamiliar abbreviations and symbols. Here are some you've already seen:

LH   Left Hand
RH   Right Hand
K   Knit
P   Purl
*   denotes where instructions begin, usually found in the phrase: rep from *.

A little experience with patterns will make them intelligible. In the meantime, we provide you with a guide to Puck's Scarf (page 32) as an introduction to what might be called Knitterese.

Puck's Scarf

Pam Allen

I love garter stitch—let me count the ways. It's easy to do. It's meditative, the true yoga stitch. It lies flat, no rolling edges. It's cushy—lots of squishy texture. It really doesn't need any kind of blocking. It looks good—I never grow tired of its ridged, rustic appearance.

A pattern often begins with an introduction. Here the designer tells you a little about the project, the inspiration, or other information that might be of interest.

Puck's Scarf

Finished measurements 6″ [15 cm] wide and 80″ [203 cm] long
*Dimensions of the completed scarf when knitted at the gauge
listed below. Gauge? Keep reading.*

Yarn Osprey by Quince & Co
Name and company of the yarn used to knit the sample.

(100% American wool; 170yd [155m]/100g)
*Fiber content of the yarn and number of yards/meters
per skein. Some patterns tell you in yards or meters how much
yarn you'll need for the project.*

2 skeins Audouin 157
Number of skeins and color used in the sample project.

Needles One pair in size US 10 [6 mm]
*"One pair" tells you that the pattern calls for two straight
needles. Circular knitting needles are joined by a cable, and if
your pattern requires a circular needle, it will tell you so. Size
US 10 [6 mm] refers to the diameter of the needle used to knit
the sample.*

Or size to obtain gauge
*This short caveat is very important. It's a reminder that
everyone knits differently, often a little looser or a little tighter
than the sample knitter. How do you know if you're spot on or
looser or tighter? Knit a gauge swatch (page 30).*

Notions Tapestry (blunt) needle
*Things other than yarn and needles that you'll need to
complete your project.*

Gauge 13 sts and 14 rows = 4″ [10 cm] in garter stitch
*This section tells you how many stitches and rows were in
the sample knitter's piece, using the EXACT yarn and needles
listed in the pattern. If you have more or fewer stitches and/
or rows, the dimensions of your final piece will vary from
the dimensions given earlier in the pattern under Finished
Measurements.*

Scarf

Here's where the step-by-step instructions begin.

Using the long-tail cast on, CO 20 sts.
*This first bit tells you two things: The number
of stitches to cast on and the cast-on method to
use. (You already know the long-tail cast on.)
Two abbreviations are used here: CO, for cast
on (page 10), and sts for stitches. To see a list of
abbreviations, go to Standard Abbreviations at
the end of the pattern in the next column.*

Row 1: (RS) Knit.

Row 2: Knit.
*After you've cast on your initial stitches, you
begin with Row 1. The pattern will tell you
whether you begin on the right side or the wrong
side of the project. Here, we begin on the right
side (RS).*

Cont in garter stitch (knit every row) until scarf
measures approx 80″ [203 cm] from beginning,
or until you have just enough yarn for binding off.
*Rows 1 and 2 establish the stitch pattern, garter
stitch. You repeat Rows 1 and 2 until the end of
your project.*

Next row: Bind off all sts.
*In the first section, we mentioned that it takes a
length of yarn about three times the width of your
knitting to bind off the last row (page 17).*

Finishing

Weave in ends. Steam- or wet-block scarf,
if desired.
*When you've finished knitting your scarf, you'll
have four tails to weave in: One at the cast on
edge, one at the bind off edge, and two in the
middle where you joined your second ball of yarn
(page 29).*

Standard abbreviations

approx	approximately
CO	cast on
cm	centimeters
cont	continue
g	grams
m	meters
mm	millimeters
RS	right side
st(s)	stitch(es)
yd	yards

Snug's Scarf

Pam Allen

A ribbed scarf is classic. For Snug's Scarf, we used a one-by-one rib; we alternated a knit stitch with a purl stitch across the row. But you could easily work a two-by-two rib for a scarf or invent your own symmetric or asymmetric pattern, for example, two knit stitches with four purl stitches. If you change the stitch pattern, all you need to adjust is the number of stitches to cast on. Ribbing draws in, so 20 stitches worked in a rib stitch will be narrower than 20 stitches worked in garter stitch (Puck's Scarf, page 32). For Snug, we cast on 31 stitches and used an uneven number of stitches so the piece begins and ends on the same kind of stitch.

Scarf length is a matter of personal preference. We like a long scarf that can easily loop around the neck. But once you've cast on and started your scarf, it's yours. End where you please!

Snug's Scarf

Finished measurements	6″ [15 cm] wide and 80″ [203 cm] long
Yarn	Osprey by Quince & Co (100% American wool; 170yd [155m]/100g) 2 skeins Kumlien's Gull 152
Needles	One pair in size US 10 [6 mm] Or size to obtain gauge
Notions	Tapestry (blunt) needle
Gauge	20 sts and 16 rows = 4″ [10 cm] in ribbing

Scarf

Using the long-tail cast on, CO 31 sts.

Row 1: (RS) *K1, p1; rep from * to last st, k1.

Row 2: *P1, k1; rep from * to last st, p1.

Cont in rib until scarf measures 80" [203 cm] from beginning, or until you have just enough yarn for binding off.

Next row: Bind off all sts in pattern (knitting the knit sts and purling the purls).

Finishing

Weave in ends. Steam- or wet-block scarf, if desired.

Standard abbreviations

approx	approximately
CO	cast on
cm	centimeters
cont	continue
k	knit
g	grams
m	meters
mm	millimeters
p	purl
rep	repeat
RS	right side
st(s)	stitch(es)
yd	yards

Yarn weights

Shown with average number of stitches over 4" and 1" (in parentheses), on appropriate size needles.

From the top (opposite page):

Fingering/sock weight:
27–32 (6¾-8) sts
US 1 to 3 [2.25 to 3.25 mm]

Sport weight:
23-26 (5¾-6½) sts
US 3 to 5 [3.25 to 3.75 mm]

DK/light worsted weight:
21-24 (5¼-6) sts
US 5 to 7 [3.75 to 4.5 mm]

Worsted/aran weight:
16-20 (4-5) sts
US 7 to 9 [4.5 to 5.5 mm]

Chunky weight:
12-15 (3-3¾) sts
US 9 to 11 [5.5 to 8 mm]

Bulky weight:
6-11 (1½-2¾) sts
US 11 and up [8 mm and up]

Needle sizes

Needle conversion chart
US size / Metric size

Needles come in different materials. Metal and plastic needles are more slippery than wooden ones. As a beginner, you may feel you have more control over what you're doing on wooden needles.

0 / 2 mm
1 / 2.25 mm
2.5 mm
2 / 2.75 mm
3 mm
3 / 3.25 mm
4 / 3.5 mm
5 / 3.75 mm
6 / 4 mm
7 / 4.5 mm
8 / 5 mm
9 / 5.5 mm
10 / 6 mm
10½ / 6.5 mm
7 mm
7.5 mm
11 / 8 mm
13 / 9 mm
15 / 10 mm
17 / 12.75 mm
19 / 15 mm
35 / 19 mm
50 / 25 mm

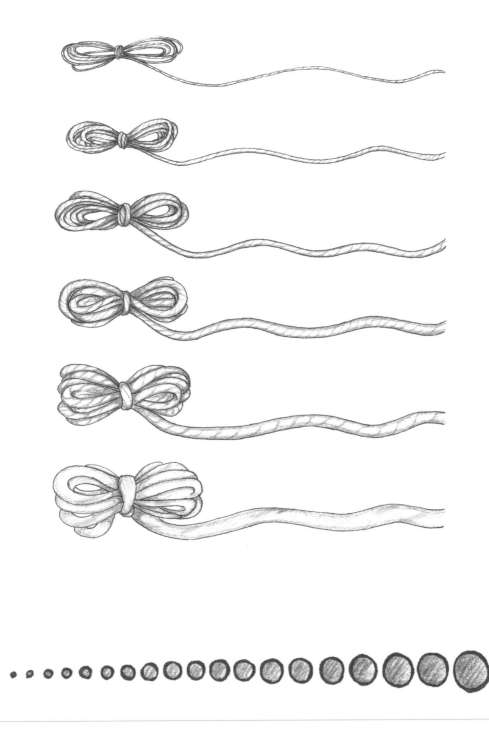

Notes

Notes

Acknowledgements

This book is the work of many hands. They are:
Dawn Catanzaro, Jerusha Robinson, and Pam Allen, who collaborated on the text,
Heather Kiernan, Mary Henley, and Dawn Catanzaro, who knitted the scarves,
Leila Raabe, who illustrated the techniques,
Pam Allen, who took the photos,
and Jennifer S. Muller who designed the book.

The instructions were tested by Lydia Larson and Kathryn Larson.

Manaan Alexander was our model.

Yarns from Quince & Co, a company sourcing wool from the US
and spinning it in American mills.

For questions and to learn more about Quince & Co,
visit us at quinceandco.com.

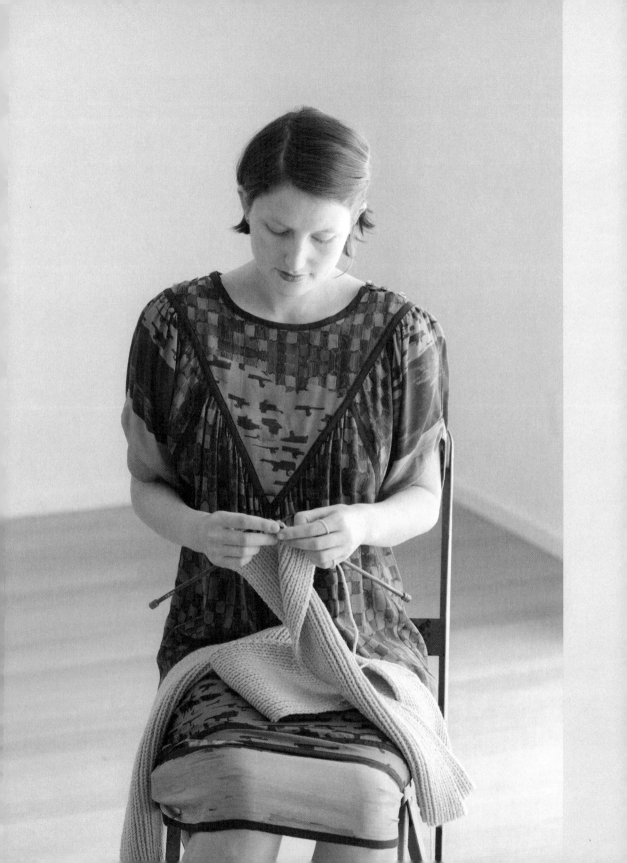